What People Are Saying About *Home Sweet Home Loan - Essential Concepts for Winning the Mortgage Game*

"Doug's book really came at a good time as I'm looking to get a new home. It has been 7 years and I know things are COMPLETELY different now than they were back then!

I discovered the timeless lessons of what I should and should not be worried about in clear, easy-to-understand English.

Bottom line, I got a lot of value from this book that will help me immensely with my new home purchase.

And, I am excited that I have the option to work with someone like Doug who actually cares about me and my family instead of just the fee he's going to be getting. He's a breath of fresh air.

Thanks Doug,"

Henry Evans, San Diego, CA   www.TimezoneMarketing.com

"As a recent client, I can confirm Doug lives up to the philosophy set forth in his book. I felt that he truly understood my goals, he answered all my questions patiently and completely, and I was thrilled with the terms of the loan I received.

Take his advice and information seriously and you should meet your goals, and have a better experience through the entire mortgage process."

David C. Frakes, MD, Cardiff-by-the-Sea, CA

"The first time I ever dealt with a bank, I wanted to have my own expert with me...maybe a parent or a friend...somebody who had "been there before". But when you buy a house, you want someone even more experienced than that—you need a pro. Make Doug Brennecke your 'wingman'. Get his book, and have him cover your back while you fight for the best mortgage you—or anyone—can get"

"Coach Gary" Micheloni, Oceanside, CA Author: "Get Paid for a Change!"

www.BestVideoWebMarketing.com

"As evidenced by his book, Doug Brennecke is passionate about helping to educate his clients about the lending process. It's a thorough and concise guide to understanding the sometimes arduous world of mortgage loans."

Harriet Baker, Encinitas, CA www.architectural-art.net

"Doug conducts business, as he writes - succinct, remarkably educational, and full of very necessary truths. His words provide transparency, years of experience, thoroughness, integrity and timeliness and are a must for anyone even remotely involved in the mortgage process...whether you are first time buyer, repeat refinancer, Realtor®, or a mortgage-broker-to-be."

Meghan Bach, Realtor®, San Diego, CA www.meghanbach.com

"This is a must read for anyone applying for a home loan! Whether you are a first time home buyer or a seasoned home owner, you will benefit and possibly even save money. Remember, money saved on a 30 year loan could be worth thousands of dollars to you! You simply can't afford to learn about the new changes in the Lending Industry when you are trying to close your loan. I have seen too many people misled over the years by inexperienced loan reps. I have worked alongside Doug for over 20 years and simply put, there is no one that I would trust more with my home loan !"

Michele Pitto, El Dorado Hills, CA www.mp4juiceplus.com

Success Stories

"I have known Doug for over 25 years. I've been a home owner for over 43 years. During that time I have bought and refinanced several homes. Over the last 20 years I have used Doug's service on both our primary residence as well as rental property. Doug has also handled both of my children's mortgage requirements. I found that Doug always was upfront about the different options available and honest about what the up front requirements were. We always sat down and asked a lot of questions of each other so we well both were comfortable while moving forward during the whole mortgage process. I have recommended Doug to several people and have received positive comments from all."

Fred Flihan, Encinitas, CA

"Doug is a wealth of information when it comes to the mortgage industry. I would never hesitate to refer a client to Doug as I know he will take care of them from beginning to end and do what it takes to get the job done! He is a pleasure to work with."

Leigh Ann Elledge, Realtor[©,] San Diego, CA

"I have financed many homes and completed refinance transactions through Doug. He is true to his craft as he does always want to first help me understand the alternatives and what to consider to make the best choice for my situation. Then he provides a solution that is complete with full transparency, something that I like considering this may be the biggest purchase I ever make. Doug gives good advice and has always been true to his word."

Dave Lehmann, San Diego, CA

"Doug really helped me through the scary and confusing process of buying a condo. He came to me and worked around my schedule, he explained things in easy to understand terms, and honestly he was kind of like a father figure to me. He was always available if I had a question or just got nervous. He's honest, he tells it like it is, and he works hard for you. There are always bumps in the road when buying property, Doug seemed to make it his mission to smooth them out."

Kelly Munson, San Diego, CA

"Doug is knowledgeable and knows his business inside out. I found him to be extremely responsible, and patient. He's great in returning calls and answering emails. I could count on him to answer questions thoroughly and quickly."

Farah Egli, Realtor©, La Jolla, CA

"In the past 15+ years, we have obtained several mortgages-all with Doug Brennecke's assistance. His professionalism is highlighted by a consistently confident, friendly and calm manner. Doug's competence is evident in the information he provides and his attention to detail in answering your questions. We've learned something new each time and have never felt as though we were rushed through a process we didn't understand. Doug Brennecke made obtaining a mortgage as enjoyable as it could be!"

Bob and Ellen Pels, San Diego, CA

Home Sweet Home Loan

Essential Concepts For Winning The Mortgage Game

Douglas J. Brennecke

Douglas J. Brennecke

1134 Calle Christopher

Encinitas, CA 92024

Doug@DougBrennecke.com

www.DougBrennecke.com

ISBN 978-0-6154-5109-1

An Incredible Free Gift For You

(Hundreds of Dollars of Free Information For You and a Special Bonus!)

Go to www.DougBrennecke.com and sign up for my special report:

"SEVEN STRATEGIES TO HELP YOU AVOID HEADACHES AND SAVE MONEY IN THE MORTGAGE PROCESS".

You will also be registered for receiving my bi-weekly electronic newsletter that provides:

- Basic mortgage education
- Thoughts and opinions on the mortgage business
- Updates on recent developments

The website provides Archived Articles, Audio, Videos, Success Stories, and Product Offerings. Take advantage of these valuable resources to help you Win The Mortgage Game!

Special Bonus: My Gift of Appreciation

When you go to the website, select the Contact Doug page and complete the web form. Provide your e-mail address and let me know that you purchased this book and I will send you a recording of a 33-minute radio interview done for "The Very Best Job In The World"!

For my wife, Sheri, who has been with me
and been supportive for my entire mortgage career,

And, to my son, Jeff, and daughter, Jenn, who have
been understanding when I needed to divide
my time to take care of my clients.

ACKNOWLEDGEMENTS

I would like to acknowledge the contribution of all my clients and prospects through the years. By asking questions and having me rise to the challenge of serving them well, they made me more congruent in my approach, more systematic in my process, and more caring as a person.

Also, I have been fortunate to have the able support of processing assistants who have helped me through my career. They have helped facilitate the transactions and have been valuable teammates in meeting my clients' needs.

And finally, this book would probably still be an unfulfilled wish if I had not met Donna Kozik and allowed her to coach me through this project.

ABOUT THE AUTHOR

Doug Brennecke began his mortgage origination career in 1977. In the four years prior, he learned the mortgage business from the servicing side, where he helped people who had already obtained their mortgage.

He has developed his expertise by working with a large savings and loan company, a small mortgage brokerage and a well-established mortgage brokerage/mortgage banking company. He is licensed by the State of California and the Nationwide Mortgage Licensing System.

In his career, he has closed nearly a half billion dollars in loans by meeting the needs of thousands of clients.

He has been featured as an Outstanding Performer in Mortgage Generator magazine, a recipient of the 2010 and 2011 Five Star Best-in-Client-Satisfaction Mortgage Professionals Award and has been contracted by attorneys for expert witness testimony.

In his career, Doug has learned that keys to success include:

Listen to the clients.
Educate them.
Tell them the truth.

CONTENTS

Chapter 1: The Person Is <u>Everything</u>   19

Chapter 2: The Good, The Bad, and The Ugly   25

Chapter 3: The Top Four Factors In the Mortgage Process   31

Chapter 4: How To Shop For Your Mortgage Loan   43

Chapter 5: Understanding the Basics: The Four C's
           Of Your Loan Request   59

Chapter 6: Mortgage Brokerage, Mortgage Banking and
           Direct Mortgage Lenders   67

Chapter 7: Avoid These 10 Costly Mortgage Mistakes   75

Chapter 8: Closing Costs and Ideas On Saving Money
           In the Mortgage Process   85

Chapter 9: The Power Of the Prequalification   95

Chapter 10: Risk-Based Pricing   101

Chapter 11: Learning From Others   107

        Final Throughts   115

        Glossary   117

INTRODUCTION

This book is for prospective borrowers who want to experience a mortgage process where they are respected for the big step they are taking, who want to know that the person with whom they are working is knowledgeable, and who want to be dealt with in a truthful manner.

In its essence, the mortgage business is a <u>people</u> business.

As mortgage originators, we are entrusted with your hopes, your dreams, your financial records, and your credit histories. At times, we are given a glimpse of the dynamics between husbands and wives, family members, and partners in business.

Because you have opened the door to your private lives, you deserve respect and courtesy and of course, confidentiality.

The mortgage process can typically take anywhere from 30 days to 90 days to complete. For this short period of time, we are working together closely in a focused interaction to accomplish your goal.

That goal is important to you, for your reasons. My role is to facilitate your reaching that goal.

It is important that I understand where you want to get to so that I can help you get there.

It is important that I communicate with you as well as I possibly can about what it takes to have you meet your goal.

I have adopted as my working philosophy the following:

~I listen to my clients.

I educate them.

I tell them the truth.~[©]

If you would like me to assist you in your home financing, I can do so in the State of California, where I am licensed.

For those who live in other states, please take my message in this book to heart and do your best to find a mortgage originator who can earn your trust and treat you with the respect that you deserve.

Chapter 1

THE PERSON IS <u>EVERYTHING</u>

The call starts out with the best of intentions:

"What are your rates and fees for …?"

The borrower wants to do their homework.

They want to get a good deal.

They don't want to overpay for the home loan.

They want to believe what they are being told.

When I receive these calls, I am concerned for the borrower. I know that in many cases they are setting themselves up for a disappointment, because their focus is on the wrong thing.

They want to feel good about getting the lowest rates and fees at the time and not leave any money on the table.

They want to believe that all loan originators are committed to telling them the truth and to tell them what they need to know.

Sadly, that is not the case.

The less scrupulous lenders out there find it easy to tell the borrower what they want to hear, and then deliver the real terms when the borrower is too deep into the transaction to make a change comfortably.

They do it by telling them "today's rates". Unless the file is already approved and ready to have the loan documents prepared, "today's rates" can't be delivered to the borrower.

They do it by quoting an interest rate, but not discussing fees.

They do it by quoting terms that may include a prepayment penalty and not mentioning it, whether that is something that is acceptable to the borrower or not.

They do it by quoting monthly payments that conveniently ignore how long the rate and payments are guaranteed. The borrower may fall in love with the low payments and not understand (until it is too late) that it is an adjustable rate loan which may or may not meet their needs.

They do it by intentionally lying about the availability of rates and programs with the hopes that they can get deep enough into the transaction so that the borrower has to accept the real terms because it is too costly to back out. Or worse, that the borrower risks losing the home they want because of the additional time it would take to make a change.

There have been efforts by Congress to create new disclosure requirements for mortgage lenders to try to prevent the abuses that have gone before.

A mortgage originator with bad intentions can always find a way to create the disclosures and still put borrowers in a bad position.

What these borrowers need to focus on is the person with whom they are

~I listen to my clients. I educate them. I tell them the truth~©

working. A good mortgage originator will ask questions before quoting rates and fees and programs.

Questions like these are important for you to receive the most reliable information from your mortgage originator:

- What is your credit score?

- How long do you intend to own the home?

- How much equity or down payment is there in the transaction?

- Are you interested in a fixed rate loan or are you open to adjustable rates?

- Would you rather keep fees as low as possible, or are you interested in a lower rate by paying loan fees?

- Can we document all of your income to qualify?

- Would you consider a prepayment fee on the loan?

- What is important to you about your home financing?

- What would be the best outcome that you could envision for this transaction?

The answers to these types of questions help the originator and the borrower create a framework for proposals and discussion.

It is a client-focused approach, with the understanding that the best possible match needs to be made between what the client wants, needs and qualify for and what is available in the mortgage market.

A good mortgage originator is willing to take the time to make sure you understand what you are getting.

A good mortgage originator is able to clearly explain how the recommended loans work, and the advantages and disadvantages of each.

A good mortgage originator is patient - understanding that obtaining the right loan is an important decision on your part.

Hearing the best terms initially from the wrong person can only lead to disappointment, headaches and higher costs.

Hearing competitive terms in a suitable program from the right person can lead to a proper decision for yourself, a comfortable process and many times a truly less costly experience. Look for the experienced, caring mortgage originator that wants to help you find a program suited to your needs.

You will remember the quality of that experience long after the close of your transaction.

Chapter 2

THE GOOD, THE BAD, AND THE UGLY

As you go through the process of mortgage application, you begin to see that there are "good, bad and ugly" representatives in the marketplace wanting your mortgage business.

It can be a very stressful time for you, because you know that the new home financing is pivotal in helping you reach your goals of completing the home purchase, improving the terms of the existing financing, or generating cash from the equity in your home to be allocated to other priorities.

In reverse order, let's list some qualities that may help you determine which category of mortgage representative you are dealing with.

Ugly:

- Does not have your best interests as a priority.

- Talks fast. Doesn't listen well.

- Wants to hurry you along to make a decision.

- Seems deliberately evasive about answering questions regarding interest rates and fees, and disclosing their own compensation.

- Wants to do as little as possible and move onto the next deal.

- Reminds you of "used car salesman" business model: "What do I have to do to get you into this mortgage product today?"

Bad:

- Does not know what may be potential problems for you situation.

- The representative is disorganized and creates confusion for you.

- Answers to your questions are unclear or incomplete.

- You have little sense of confidence that they know what they are doing.

- Gives you the impression that they will take your loan request and "throw it against the wall to see if it will stick".

Good:

- Asks probing questions and listens well.

- Wants to discover what is important to you and what your best outcome would be, if possible.

- Is able to explain advantages and disadvantages of various programs of interest.

- Is able to explain loan programs so that they are understandable to you.

- Answers questions directly about how they are paid and gives a guideline for their fee for service.

- Can explain what the various fees are for, and which may be negotiable.

- Helps you understand where your request is strong, and what aeas may require particular attention.

- Explains the process so you always know what the next step is.

- Inspires confidence that you are being cared for and that they have your best interests in mind.

Shopping for a mortgage loan can be a tricky game.

You want to get the best terms that you can, and you also want to be provided quality service. The lenders that "sell" rates often will publish advertisements that are designed to get their phones to ring. The rates that are published may not even be valid by the time they make it to print.

If your focus is entirely on the lowest rate, you will encounter the "ugly" representative that will say or do whatever they need to do to get your business in the door, and then you will be faced with market reality (meaning that the rate they advertised is not available to you and then they present the "real rates"). The revelation of the higher rates will come at a time when you don't have alternatives to make a change.

When you start to focus on the service-oriented representative you will encounter both the "bad" and the "good". There are many new representatives in the mortgage business. They are eager to please and they have pleasant personalities. They are very likeable. But, they may not be very knowledgeable and their lack of experience may contribute to a horrendous outcome for you.

You may find that they were not aware of program requirements, adjustments to the interest rate/fee pricing model, terms of the new mortgage that affect your qualifications, your costs, or the suitability of the loan for you.

You need to find those "good" representatives that tell you the straight story from the beginning, that know the guidelines and requirements and can escort you through the home loan process with care, proper counsel and at a cost to you that is fair.

You want to be well-served so that you make a proper decision for your family; so that you don't have to worry about putting food on the table because of your mortgage payment, and that the loan fits into a plan for you to save for your future and your children's futures.

Chapter 3

THE TOP FOUR FACTORS IN THE MORTGAGE PROCESS

In a 2008 survey conducted with mortgage borrowers, there were four factors that were determined as the most important.

In order of importance, they were:

1. Communication.
2. Integrity.
3. A Smooth and Complete Process.
4. Competitive Products and Rates.

Let's take a look at each of these and how they fit together to help you have the best possible experience in obtaining your new home loan.

COMMUNICATION

It has often been said that most people can deal with what needs to be done, if they are only told what the rules are.

In the mortgage lending field, it is so important to know what to expect, how the process works and the details of the specific proposals that you are asked to consider.

Your mortgage originator should be able to tell you the steps and timing of their application process. From the initial interview or submission of the loan application, you should understand the time line for obtaining the credit report, appraisal, escrow and title paperwork, verifications of income and asset and for the submission of the loan file for approval.

From there, you should know the turn-around time on a submitted file in the lender's underwriting process. If the file has been put together well and is complete, there should not be many conditions to be satisfied on the loan approval prior to the lender preparing the final loan documents.

Once the loan documents are signed and returned to the lender, you will need to know how long it takes for the lender to do their final quality control and to authorize the funding of the loan to complete the transaction.

In addition to these procedural and timing expectations, your mortgage originator should also be able to explain how their process ties together with the escrow company, the title company, your home inspector and termite clearance, and the appraiser.

They also need to be mindful of the specifics of your contract, so that they can meet any deadlines that have been agreed upon by you and the seller. For instance, in California, there is a common clause in the contract that calls for the buyer to remove their financing contingency within 17 days of the seller's acceptance. It is imperative that you have a mortgage originator who gets the paperwork started quickly, who puts a quality loan package together and gets a loan approval that has few conditions.

When you are asked to remove your financing contingency and put your earnest money deposit at risk, you want to be as sure as you possibly can that there is not something to prevent you from obtaining your home loan.

And, of course, you need a mortgage originator who can listen, who can understand what is important to you, who understands your risk tolerances and time horizons, so that the loan programs that are presented to you are suitable matches for you qualifications and needs.

It takes an experienced professional to present options to you that are clear and thorough. You want someone who can speak in language that you understand and makes sure that you are comfortable with the final recommendations. You will also want to have someone who can point out the positives of various loan programs, and any negatives as well, so that you can make an informed decision.

INTEGRITY

There are so many opportunities in the mortgage industry for a person of low integrity to make a handsome living and not serve their clients well.

As mentioned previously, a person who wants to distort some timelines, some facts, some attributes of loan programs – and we haven't yet talked about rates and fees - to draw a borrower to them, has plenty of chances.

The best advice I can give is modeled after Ronald Reagan's statement of

"Trust, but verify".

If a mortgage originator makes representations, find out how you can get some additional information to support the statements. You can request a copy of the credit report, a confirmation from an escrow officer or appraiser that things were done in the timely manner promised, or a copy of the final loan approval that outlines all of the conditions of the loan approval. There are ways that you can be more assured that your loan request is on track to be completed as proposed and in the time frame that you expect.

In my opinion, integrity and communication go hand-in-hand.

If you have your mortgage originator go through the steps of the application process and the escrow process and the details of the various mortgage programs, you will get an excellent idea of the integrity of the person with whom you are dealing.

If the mortgage originator is unskilled, they may honestly answer "I don't know, but I will find out". If they try to bluff their way through an answer, you will probably be able to detect irregularities in what they have said, and that may point to an integrity issue.

If you are trying to understand details and you keep getting vague answers in return, that may also point to an integrity issue. It may be an unwillingness to give you the correct information that is not favorable to their outcome.

If you find that a particular loan program is being touted that does not seem to be suitable to you, you need to understand whether that is the only solution that they have. If there are additional choices, the presentation of an unsuitable product may point to an integrity issue.

In my opinion, the more transparent the mortgage originator is regarding how the process works, how the programs work, how much you are paying in fees and who receives those, and the willingness to admit if you have better choices elsewhere goes a long way to proving their integrity.

Be sure to ask around about the person you are working with, or to ask for referrals and testimonials from happy clients and real estate agents. A person who has been originating loans for a long time, and who has happy repeat and referral clients says a lot about them being a "straight shooter".

A SMOOTH AND COMPLETE PROCESS

We've already alluded to this, especially in the Communication section, but a skilled mortgage originator knows how to put a package together and how to anticipate foreseeable problems.

It all starts with the loan application and collection of supporting paperwork. I still prefer to interview my clients whenever possible, and meeting them in person is the best way to get things started.

In an efficient one hour meeting we can go through the data gathering and really probe as to what is important to you. Knowing this information allows me to brainstorm solutions to your individual situation and to strategize about making your home ownership dreams come true.

I have developed systems that allow me to make a comprehensive request for supporting paperwork that fits their profile. It could be paystubs, W-2 forms, tax returns, bank and brokerage statements, retirement account information, divorce or bankruptcy paperwork, or explanatory letters regarding special situations. Getting all of this information up-front, rather than going back repeatedly to the borrower for yet another piece of paper, is integral to a smooth process.

There are situations that arise that are not foreseeable, and we all need to make allowances for that possibility. This has been even more true recently as the mortgage industry tries to get back to more conservative underwriting of loan files. However, there are many obstacles that need to be recognized and discussed and strategized about.

A smooth process is also a result of knowledge, experience, skill, communication and integrity.

COMPETITIVE PRODUCTS AND RATES

Surprisingly to many people, this is not at the top of the list.

It is surprising because so many borrowers call up for information and the only thing that they are interested in is "What are your rates?"

Accepting a direct answer to that question is naive on the borrower's part. There are so many factors that go into determining the right program for a borrower, and the interest rate and fees to be quoted, that the information provided is not appropriate or possibly a deliberate lie.

In order to do a good job for our clients, and to treat them properly, we need to remember an old adage:

Prescription without diagnosis is malpractice.

Simply put, if we don't ask the proper questions and just offer a "one size fits all" solution, we are not doing the best thing for our clients.

We should know if the new property is going to be their home and how long they intend to own it.

Are they salaried or self-employed?

Do they qualify by proving all of their income, or do we need to research other alternatives.

What are the credit scores?

What is the purchase price, how much down payment, and is any of it coming from a gift?

In addition to the new housing debts, how much do they owe in other obligations?

These are some of the questions that are important to know the answers to so that a proper loan program and accurate interest rate and fee quote can be presented.

I know that I have lost the opportunity to help a lot of borrowers because when they shop rates and fees only, the person that tells them the lowest numbers will get the opportunity to do the business. By taking the time to fully understand their situation and providing a proper quote, it is often not the lowest that they will hear. But it is the correct quote for them.

The mortgage originators who deliberately deceive a borrower to get the loan application process started with them know that there will be a point where the borrower will continue with them despite what the final terms are. And the final terms are almost never the low quoted rates produced at the beginning.

The pain of starting a new application process with someone new and the time that it takes will jeopardize most purchase transactions. And the deceptive originators know this. And the borrowers usually fold. And the borrowers develop the thought that all mortgage originators are the same, so what difference does it make?

Nothing could be further from the truth – all mortgage originators are not the same.

The survey answers provide a solid basis for anyone shopping for a new home loan.

The programs and rates need to be competitive, but they will rarely be the lowest. Getting the lowest rates is more good fortune than by scientific design.

If the process is not smooth and complete, it will leave you with a bad feeling - possibly forever.

If you are working with someone without integrity, there is no basis for anything else working well.

And if communication is poor or non-existent, you can expect nothing but problems in all areas of the transaction.

Getting a home loan is a big decision. You have a lot to lose if you don't try to maximize these four factors when you decide with whom you want to work.

Chapter 4

HOW TO SHOP FOR YOUR MORTGAGE LOAN

In speaking with clients and potential clients, I find that borrowers' approaches to researching their mortgage alternatives range from a well-directed process to a sincere, but ineffective procedure.

Some of these borrowers are willing to accept guidance to help them achieve their goals. Others forge ahead stubbornly, thinking they are on the right path, but may reach their goals only by being lucky.

Please use the following outline as a way to conduct your mortgage research. Also, please understand that these steps are fluid in nature, and that you will pick up important information throughout the process. Don't think that you have to complete one step before starting another.

1. Know your outcome.

I often ask my clients, "If things go exactly as you would like, what would that result look like?"

With all of the details that they have to consider, they may have never thought about that before.

But, it is important to know what your goals are.

The outcome that you define can be aided by answering these types of questions.

How long will you be owning this home? Your answers may be influenced by being a first-time buyer, a move-up buyer, or settling in for the bulk of your adult lives. Also, how long your children will be in a particular school district often helps decide this question. Career plans come into play as well.

How long would you anticipate having this mortgage in place? This may be a much different question than the first one. You may need an initial home loan that gives you immediate benefits but is not designed for the long-term. You may be anticipating additional funds that will allow you to pay down, or pay off the loan after it is created.

What is your risk tolerance? Would you rather consider loans that will never change, but whose interest rate and payments may be slightly higher, or consider loans that provide a lesser element of stability and offer lower rates and payments?

How much of your available funds do you want to invest? You may want to put as much down payment as possible to keep your loan balance and payments low. Or you may want to put little down, keep your funds more liquid, and use leverage of a higher loan amount.

How much do you want to budget for the housing expense: mortgage payment, property taxes, insurance and/or homeowner's fees? There are many times that you may be able to obtain loan approval for a higher monthly payment than what you are comfortable with. I never want to over-obligate you, and this question allows us to get the topic on the table so we can have a frank discussion.

As you might guess, your perfect outcome may not be compatible with lending guidelines.

It is very gratifying to hit your target! And when you can't, you know where the adjustments are being made and why they are necessary or recommended.

2. Be realistic.

As you talk with the various lenders and gather information, you are going to be getting some feedback as to what is possible for your situation.

Your better loan representatives will be able to discuss lender guidelines and educate you as to what is approvable in today's market.

In early 2007, we were in an entirely different lending environment. Loans approaching 100% of the value of the home, that allowed for approval without verification of income and/or assets, or certain more exotic loan products were readily available then. But not now.

If you are hearing of your neighbor's or co-worker's loan experience, it's important to understand that each borrower's profile is unique, and it is to be assessed in light of the lending guidelines at the time.

Even now, originators are experiencing something of a moving target with regard to guidelines. As investors have left the market, lenders have had to change the guidelines for the types of loans that they will originate.

Sometimes, this happens in the middle of a transaction we are processing for a client. We can do our research, get the loan request started, and by the time we are ready to submit the loan to the lender, the guidelines have changed.

If you had decided to apply with a direct lender and this happened, you would have to start all over again with a new lender, possibly having to pay for additional appraisals and credit reports.

If you were with a mortgage broker like me, your application, appraisal and credit report can be directed to a different lender with compatible guidelines to your situation.

It is important to remember that your loan application is not a redemption coupon, but it is a request for the lender to consider and hopefully approve.

It is always great when the process goes smoothly and there are no big surprises. But, be prepared for some obstacles to surface and work with people that you know are giving you information that is researched to the best of their abilities.

Topics 3, 4, and 5 are pieces of a puzzle that will help you pull a workable picture together.

3. Choosing a lender.

You need to do proper research to make your best decision. But how do you know who to trust for solid information?

I suggest that you get recommendations from people you know who have more experience or who know the reliable players in the local market.

Your real estate agent may have some recommendations or be able to tell you of their experience with someone you mention. Many times they will refer you to a mortgage company that is associated with their real estate company.

There is nothing inherently wrong with that, but be aware that there is a potential financial benefit to the real estate company if you work with their lender.

Ask your work associates if they had a good experience with their lender and get recommendations from them.

Treat print ads and radio ads with the understanding that those ads are designed to get the lender's phone to ring. If they are quoting interest rates, realize that the quotes may be outdated by the time you respond.

Some lenders deliberately promote very low rates, knowing that they won't have to deliver them, but giving them the opportunity to start the process with you. Reality is presented at a later date, sometimes when it is too late for you to make a change.

You should get 3-5 solid recommendations from your trusted sources and from your own research.

As you make your research calls, think of it as an interview process. You are going to do the hiring of a loan originator to help you reach your goal.

Gathering loan data will be important, but I would recommend that you also focus on the manner in which your questions are answered, and how helpful, considerate, and caring the originator is.

Does the originator:

A. Return your calls in a reasonable period of time?

B. Ask lots of questions to make sure that they understand your situation, or do they offer a solution before diagnosing what is appropriate?

C. Have a limited array of loan products that they try to fit you into, or are they taking your needs and qualifications to find the best match from the marketplace?

D. Give you a feeling of transparency about the transaction? You deserve straight answers to your questions so that you can make an informed decision that serves you well.

As you talk to several lenders, you will learn some new things as you go along. If you can ascertain a "red flag" that may be troublesome, make sure you ask about that with each lender. How each one answers that question may give you important insights about with whom you want to work.

4.   Deciding on a loan product.

As you speak with various lenders, you are going to get some ideas about loan products that are both appropriate for your situation, and that may be approvable under current guidelines.

Unfortunately, sometimes the loan that best fits your needs may not be available based on your qualifications.

Factors that affect that availability can include:

A. Credit scores and credit history.

B. Stability of employment, or self-employment.

C. Stability and adequacy of income.

D. Property considerations.

E. Amount of down payment.

F. Amount of cash reserves after closing.

G. Percentage of monthly obligations in relation to your income.

I would suggest that as you gather information from your loan originator prospects, you also get their top 2 or 3 loan product recommendations.

These recommendations should be based on their complete understanding of your situation, your needs, your goals and their interpretation of current underwriting guidelines.

Have them state their case as to why they think these are appropriate loan choices for you. Again, this type of discussion allows you to determine the quality of the originator. Are they trying to make the best match for you based on your needs, or are they just trying to sell you a loan?

If you have 3-5 potential lenders and each of them offer 2-3 loan program choices to you, you will probably find that there are at least 3-5 loan programs that end up receiving high recommendations over and over. Hopefully, these 3-5 choices will also be ones that you find acceptable, and you can narrow your focus to the rates and fees.

5. Assessing rates and costs.

The mortgage market is dynamic.

It is not uncommon for the 25-30 lenders with whom I work to offer rates first thing in the morning, and as the money markets unfold during the day, to make adjustments up or down to reflect the market activity.

To give yourself, and your loan originator finalists, the best opportunity to get accurate information you should get quotes from each of them on the same day, and hopefully all in the morning or all in the afternoon.

You should know how long your proposed escrow period is going to be. If you are purchasing, it will be stipulated in your purchase contract. If you are refinancing, it may be based on how long the lender needs to work their way through your file after it rises to the top of their incoming business.

Let's say that the escrow period will be 45 days. You need to ask each of your lenders what the rate and fee quote would be if you locked that day for a 45-day period. Rate locks are often offered for 15-, 30-, 45- and 60-day periods.

You have to compare apples to apples to avoid misunderstandings and confusion.

Through your initial conversations with the loan originators, you should have had the opportunity to explore the comparisons of interest rate quotes with zero points, 1/2 point, 1 point, and maybe 2 points. Make sure that all of your originators are quoting based on the same terms.

In addition to the loan origination fees, ask specifically what other loan-related fees will be charged by that lender. These may include loan processing fees, administrative fees, and document preparation fees.

Other fees that will be part of your closing costs will include escrow fees, title fees, appraisal, credit report costs, notary/sign-up fees, and pro-rations of interest, taxes, and insurance. For the most part, these costs will be the same no matter which lender you select. But be clear on all of your anticipated charges, and make sure to understand which ones end up with your lender.

You can see that these three steps give you an opportunity to interview and gather information, with you circling in on your final choice.

If you are diligent about including all of these recommendations in your search pattern, I think that you will discover the right person with whom to work, and you will give yourself an opportunity to feel confident that you are make good decisions.

There are a couple of other items that would be important to assess as you do your loan research:

A.Understand the trade-off between paying a higher interest rate and zero points vs. paying a lower interest rate and some points.

When you are offered a zero-point loan, you need to realize that you are not getting something for free.

A lender may be willing to create a loan for you without requiring you to pay discount points (a fee designed to "buy-down" the interest rate) or to pay origination points (a fee designed to pay the mortgage originator for their services).

The lender will absorb the cost of paying the origination fee, but they will charge you, the borrower, a slightly higher interest rate for doing so.

Let's take a look at an example based on a loan amount of $300,000; 30-year fixed rate of 6.625% with zero points, or 30-year fixed rate of 6.375% with a loan fee of 1 point.

Payments at 6.625% will be $1,920.93. Payments will be lowered to $1,871.61 at the 6.375% rate, but it will cost you $3,000.00 to obtain the lower rate (1% of the loan amount = 1 point.)

If you compare the 1/4% reduction of interest rate vs. the cost, it would take you 4 years to recoup your investment of the 1 point fee.

If you compare the difference in payments of $49.32 per month to the cost of $3,000.00, you will calculate that it will take almost 61 months to recover the 1 point cost.

So, if you have the resources to pay the loan fee, and you plan on keeping the loan in place for at least 4-5 years, it would be wise to go with the lower interest rate. After the break-even points, all the benefits of the lower interest rate will work in your favor.

Whenever you are offered choices of interest rates and loan fees, you should do a similar analysis so that you have a good idea of the wisdom of paying a higher interest rate, or paying higher loan fees.

It is an important consideration as you finalize the terms of your loan so that it is suitable for you based on your time horizons.

B. Be sure to ask about whether there will be a prepayment fee on your loan.

A prepayment fee, also known as a prepayment penalty, is a clause included in your loan contract that allows the lender to charge an additional fee if you pay the loan off within the first three or five years, (depending on the clause).

The typical clause allows you to pay up to 20% of the original loan amount each year without paying any prepayment fee. If you should pay more than the 20%, or pay the loan in full – which is much more likely - you would be subject to paying 6 months interest on the amount over the 20%.

Let's do a calculation bases on a loan amount of $300,000 at 6.625%.

You would be allowed to pay 20%, that is $60,000, with no penalty. If you paid the loan in full, the remaining $240,000 would be subject to a 6 month's interest charge.

Your prepayment fee would be $240,000 times 6.625% (.06625), which gives you the annual interest, divided by 2, which gives you the figure for 6 months. $240,000 x .06625 / 2 = $7,950.00.

If you even think that there is a likelihood that you will pay off the loan within the prescribed 3- or 5-year period, you would be much better negotiating the prepayment fee away at the beginning of the transaction.

Although each loan program may offer different terms, a good rule of thumb may be that it would cost you 1/4 point more in the loan fees at origination to keep the prepayment clause out of your loan contract.

The math becomes very simple at this point. Pay $750 more at loan origination (1/4 of 1% of $300,000) to avoid any possibility of paying as much as $7,950.00 if you were to pay off the loan early.

If you are convinced, however, that you will keep the loan beyond the 3- or 5-year period, you can save the additional fee at loan origination and never have to deal with the prepayment fee either.

Ask lots of questions of your mortgage representative.

Make sure that they explain things so that you can understand them. If they are unable to clearly communicate the concepts and the math, you are facing a situation where the loan product may not be providing the benefits that you expect.

Chapter 5

UNDERSTANDING THE BASICS: THE FOUR C's OF YOUR LOAN REQUEST

Many borrowers find the loan process bewildering and confusing. It doesn't help when those of us who are in the business use verbal shorthand and jargon that separates you from understanding what is going on and what your loan product will do for you.

The creation of your loan, and its approval are a combination of four basic moving parts. I learned them as the Four C's: Cash, Credit, Capacity, and Collateral. When lenders design programs and establish the pricing of the loan (interest rate plus loan fees), they are assessing the layers of risk associated with each of these categories.

Let's take a look at each of them.

Cash:

The lender wants to know that you have enough money to provide for your down payment for the purchase of the home, you can pay for your closing costs, and that you have some level of cash reserves after the closing.

They primarily would like to see that you have the funds from your own ability to save and grow your liquid assets.

As part of your loan file, we have to document how much you have in liquid assets, show the sources, and show that they are "seasoned". If sizable deposits appear in your accounts shortly before closing, the lender will be concerned that the new money is also borrowed.

In certain circumstances, you may be able to obtain a gift from family members, which we would need to document as a gift and not a loan. And, the lenders will give you credit for a percentage of the value of your retirement funds (IRA, 401(k), 403(b), etc.).

If you are refinancing, they will want to see that you have suitable balances for closing costs and reserves.

Credit:

Until the advent and acceptance of credit scoring, the lender would review the credit report and make an assessment as to the paying habits, the types of credit the borrower had (mortgage, auto loans, credit cards, student loans, finance companies, charge-offs, collections), and whether they were prudent users or abusers of credit. It was a combination of objective and subjective analysis, and was more art than science.

The credit scoring systems now take all of these factors into account in a "black box" analysis and produce a score. Because each of the three credit repositories use proprietary systems, they don't publish exactly how their scores are produced. There are websites that will allow you to subscribe and do "what if?" scenarios if you are interested in pursuing a program to improve your credit score.

Although the lenders use the credit score to fit your loan request into a risk-based pricing tier, the underwriters will not rely only on the score and disregard the rest of the credit history. They will make sure that your recent payment habits are acceptable in addition to considering the credit scoring models.

Capacity:

This refers to your ability to pay the monthly payments.

The two primary areas of interest are employment stability and that your income is sufficient to support the proposed new mortgage debt, taxes and insurance, homeowner's association fees, and all your consumer credit obligations.

As a general rule, lenders are looking for continuous employment in the same job or line of work of at least two years. Also, they like to see that the sum of those monthly obligations listed above fit within about 40% of your gross monthly income if you are salaried or a wage-earner. The percentage mentioned above (also known as debt-to-income ratio) is based on guidelines that change periodically and are specified for each loan product (fixed rate, adjustable rate, etc.).

If you are self-employed or earn commissions, the lenders will do their analysis based on your gross income less business expenses. This calculation gives them an idea of your net business income that they equate to your personal income, and it puts you on an equal footing with the salaried person and wage-earner.

Collateral:

A real estate loan is secured by a piece of property. The lender ultimately wants to have their loan secured so that if you don't make your payments, they have the ability to recover the unpaid balance of the loan through a foreclosure proceeding.

This is why the lenders require an appraisal of the home, so that they can feel comfortable that their loan is well-secured.

Lending guidelines change and risk assessments differ when the property is owner-occupied or a rental, if it is a detached home, a condominium, or if it is in a planned-unit development. Rural properties and unimproved land and lots present even more stringent criteria.

The underwriters are using their judgment and their understanding of the lender's guidelines to make an assessment about approving your loan application. They do have the authority to approve loans outside of guidelines if there are good reasons for doing so. We call this rationale "compensating factors".

As an example, if your debt-to-income ratio was higher than the guideline figure, but you have substantial cash reserves after closing, they could justify approving the loan.

The argument could be that if you were in a pinch periodically on the monthly outgo, you had more than enough cash reserves to supplement your income in an emergency.   It is a strength in your file that "compensates" for a weakness in another area.

When you are shopping for a mortgage, and the representative gives you a quote without exploring these variables with you, the information you are receiving has a high chance of being erroneous. Know with whom you are working and that they are taking care to provide you with accurate information so that you are not encouraged to begin the process with false expectations and to be presented with the real terms at a later date.

Chapter 6

MORTGAGE BROKERAGE, MORTGAGE BANKING, AND DIRECT MORTGAGE LENDERS

As you work with representatives who facilitate your requests for home loans, there are a several different ways your interests can be represented.

Mortgage brokers serve as an advocate for you, the borrower, with the lender. They have access to lenders and programs that you as a borrower are unable to find on your own and in many cases they can also work with the more prominent lenders on your behalf.

They should help you complete the mortgage application, educate you as to available loan programs and costs, and counsel you on any concerns and possible solutions that could affect your loan approval.

The lenders make their loan products available to them through what lenders call their wholesale division. It is called that because they offer their interest rates and fees at a "wholesale" price to the mortgage brokers and allow the brokers to earn their compensation for the work they do.

When lenders create loans directly, that is commonly called their retail operation. The rates and fees that they charge are competitive with what is charged by mortgage brokers. They then pay their staff for the work that they do for the lenders as employees.

So, you should find that the quotes you receive from the lenders directly or through mortgage brokers to be very similar. If that were not the case, one or the other would not be able to compete and would cease to be a player in the mortgage market.

When you complete an application with a mortgage broker, they will put together a package for your loan request and select as many potential lending prospects as possible.

If your qualifications are strong and many lenders will be willing to approve your loan, the mortgage broker can select among the lowest in price - that is, interest rate and loan fee - to get you the best terms possible.

The big advantage of this approach is that one loan application with a mortgage broker opens you to the market of available loan products that they represent.

Based on their knowledge, experiences and resources, they package your loan for presentation to the lender. They do not have any direct ability to approve your loan, but should be well-versed in the guidelines for your loan request and can often persuasively influence the underwriter to approve your loan if there are differences of opinion. The lender will approve the loan, draw the loan documents, and fund the loan.

If they are unable to gain approval with Lender A they can take the same package that they have put together and submit the request to Lenders B, C, D, etc. if necessary to work toward approval.

Although it may be maddening at times to have brokers give so many different opinions and viewpoints when it comes to getting your loan approved, it is also the major advantage that they have in helping you.

If every lender gave them the same answer at all times, there would be no need to have multiple sources with which to place your loan request. So, having some lenders who will say "yes" when others say "no" is actually a good thing, and we do our best to find the "yes" lenders as early in the process as possible.

If you have a borrower profile that limits the choices, it will probably be necessary to have your loan file submitted to any number of lenders who provide loan products that fill a particular niche.

A mortgage broker is a very valuable resource for you. Their experience, their knowledge, and their ability to match your qualifications to the available loan products saves you time and trouble, and they can offer you competitive rates and fees.

In addition to mortgage brokerage, you also have the availability of lenders who offer **mortgage banking.**

Mortgage banking is distinct from mortgage brokerage because the mortgage banking operation allows them to have your loan underwritten, loan documents prepared, and the funding of your loan all under the control of the originating company.

In this case, they have a select number of lender relationships, usually up to about 10, that are known as correspondent lenders.

This means that their company has developed the trust and the relationship with these lenders for them to make the loan decision on behalf of the lender.

The mortgage banking company has arranged for lines of credit to create these loans. These are commonly known as warehouse lines, because after the loan is funded they are "warehoused" until the lender for whom the loan was created purchases it off the warehouse line from the originating company.

Being able to offer loans within a correspondent lending relationship gives the originating company the added ability to have your file move more efficiently through the process. They have more access to the underwriter, the document preparation person and the funder of the loan to try to facilitate special situations or timing issues.

In today's lending environment, many companies that were previously able to offer mortgage banking have had to give it up because their warehouse lines of credit have not been renewed. Being able to maintain these lines of credit requires frequent re-qualification, and as the mortgage business hit so many obstacles in the last couple of years, a lot of companies could not maintain their qualifications.

In both mortgage brokerage and mortgage banking, once your loan application is in process, the originating lenders have the ability to get electronic loan approval through the correspondent lenders. They submit the data from your file, the automated underwriting system renders its decision and they receive a list of conditions that must be satisfied to finalize the approval.

The list of conditions will include the lender's review of the physical file so that they can validate the data that was submitted. The approval will typically notify them of the maximum interest rate up to which the approval is valid.

Because underwriting guidelines have tightened recently, it is in your best interest to complete a loan application early in your time frame for wanting to purchase or refinance. This early action on your part will allow the lender to get the preliminary loan approval, and to have a list of conditions from the lender that are to be satisfied.

When the time becomes right - either the right home you want to purchase presents itself, or when loan pricing is where you want it to be - you can then be in a position to move quickly on your request.

And, you will already know just what the lenders are looking for to avoid surprises.

Direct mortgage lenders are typically the big banks that have extensive branch networks. They are in competition with mortgage brokers and mortgage bankers, but most of them offer a mortgage lending channel through their wholesale and/or correspondent divisions.

If you applied with the one retail lender, your request will need to fit into that lender's available loan programs and underwriting pattern. The representative working there will be asking you to adapt exclusively to their policies.

If that lender were to say "no", you would have to generate a new loan request with another lender. This would take significantly more time and effort on your part, since you would have to regenerate the loan application repetitively. Also, you may have additional fees for duplicate appraisals of the home since most retail lenders do not find another lender's appraisals acceptable.

As always, measure the quality of the interactions with representatives from all your lender choices. You are looking for lending partners that will take your needs seriously and will work hard to match the appropriate loan recommendation to your needs.

Give yourself every advantage to have your financing of your home go smoothly. Give yourself lots of choices, lots of flexibility, and be proactive in the process.

Chapter 7

AVOID THESE 10 COSTLY MORTGAGE MISTAKES

The mortgage process can be overwhelming and confusing at times. Lending programs and qualifications change frequently, and there are many "moving parts". When you take into account the properties, credit histories, employment and income, the capacity of the borrower to make payments, and the knowledge and biases that the borrowers and the mortgage representative bring to the process, you can see that making the right match of a loan product to a borrower can be more an art than a science.

By avoiding these mistakes, you can save time and money:

Mistake No. 1: Not doing your homework.

Especially if you are a first-time buyer, you need to do enough research to understand the mortgage lending process. The fact that you are reading this book tells me that you are interested in being knowledgeable.

With so much general information on the internet, you have opportunities to get an idea of how all the pieces fit together. However, I would never recommend that you rely solely on internet sources for your information.

If you are a repeat buyer, or if you are interested in refinancing, you will already have an idea of how the mortgage process works, but it will still be worthwhile for you to re-acquaint with the most recent procedures, time-lines, documentation requirements, etc. This is especially true since the lending industry has gone from very liberal to very conservative in its underwriting and paperwork guidelines.

Failure to do this homework can cost you time and money due to delays, or paying too much for a loan product without knowing what is available in the marketplace.

Rely on a trusted mortgage professional to help you. They can assist you by asking a series of questions that will help you define your goals, and to help you determine a game plan to follow.

Mistake No. 2: Not knowing what is on your credit report.

This is one thing that you don't want to leave to chance, or to the last minute. Credit scoring has become such a big part of the mortgage process, that not knowing if your report is accurate, and not knowing what your credit score is puts you at a huge disadvantage.

There are several on-line sources to get your credit report. But more importantly, you will want to make sure that you get scores from all three repositories: Equifax, TransUnion and Experian. It is not uncommon for one repository to have information that another does not. If you only access one and think that it is representative, you may be surprised later.

The typical lending guideline is to use the middle of the three scores as being representative. There may be additional requirements that you have at least 3-4 tradelines that are reporting as active in the last 24 months. Although it is not necessarily negative, lack of credit can be a big obstacle because the lender has no idea of your ability to meet ongoing commitments.

Mistake No. 3: Not understanding mortgage products.

You need to make sure that the loan product you are intending to put into place is right for you. There are literally hundreds of different loan programs and they are designed to fulfill the needs of different segments of the market. Not all of the loans that you see advertised are going to be compatible with your qualifications or your needs and goals.

A big problem that I see is that borrowers do not match their time horizons and risk tolerance to the loan product. They may be tempted to pay a higher interest rate than is necessary by getting a 30-year fixed-rate loan, when a loan that is fixed for 3, 5, or 7 years (which typically carry lower interest rates) could match up with their timeline for ownership.

Another potential problem could be that the loan has a prepayment clause that costs thousands of dollars when the borrower wants to pay off the loan early. Knowing how long you intend to own the home is a big factor in making the right match for you.

Also, whenever you consider an adjustable rate loan, you need to fully understand how the rate changes, when it changes, how much it can change, how much the payments would be when it changes and what the worst-case scenario could look like.

Your loan representative should be able to let you know the advantages and disadvantages of the loan products that you are considering for your situation, and in a style that allows you to understand.

Mistake No. 4: Not understanding loan pricing.

The rates and fees that you are quoted can change without notice, often several times in a day.

When you shop for a loan, you need to understand that the rate and fee combination is designed to provide the lender a calculated yield. When I use the term "pricing", I am referring to this rate and fee combination.

If you want to keep the interest rate low, you will most likely be asked to pay loan fees, commonly known as "points" (1 point equals 1% of the loan amount) to achieve that yield calculation for the lender. If you want to keep your loan fees low, you may need to accept a slightly higher interest rate.

If you don't match the interest rate and fee combination with your time line for keeping the mortgage in place, you risk overpaying in one way or the other. Make sure that the loan pricing is designed to meet your goals.

Mistake No. 5: Not getting pre-approved for home shopping.

You want to put yourself in the best position for having your offer to purchase accepted by the seller.

One of the best ways to do this is to complete a loan application, and have the lender provide a conditional loan approval for you, subject to an acceptable home appraisal. When your offer is presented, you and your agent can provide this evidence of pre-approval. The seller will be more confident that there will be fewer surprises through the escrow period, and give you a better chance of buying the home.

If you don't do this, you risk missing the home you really want, and in a fast-moving market, finding a comparable home can be more expensive. Working with your lender to get you pre-approved so you can move forward with confidence is time well-spent.

Mistake No. 6: Not knowing who is offering the "lowest rate".

I put "lowest rate" in quotes for a reason. I see the results of this too often.

A borrower has been promised a rate lower than the prevailing market rates, and chooses to apply with that lender. Most of the time, it is a lender that places prominent advertising, and is not a referral to the borrower.

At the beginning, everything looks good, and all the right things are said by the lender's representative. When the approval comes through, and there are very few days left before the close of escrow, the bombshell hits. The rate is no longer available, the rate was not locked in as promised, or the investor/lender is approving the loan under a different program that does not honor the initial rate quote.

At this point, the borrower feels that they have no choice but to close at the higher terms, otherwise they are risking being able to buy their home. The net result is that the lender who misleads the borrower is rewarded with the business, and the borrower typically ends up with the market rates that were quoted by the more ethical lenders.

There have been new disclosure requirements implemented with the intent of lessening this type of activity. But it comes back to the person you are working with. Feel comfortable with the integrity level of your representative.

Very rarely are there extraordinarily low rates available – it is a very competitive marketplace, and the funds for loans are procured through auctions of mortgage money that all the major lenders access to have a

---

continual supply of funds.

Mistake No. 7: Not seeing the rate lock in writing.

This ties together with knowing the lender with whom you are working. If you are working with a lender that is a referral, and their services have been recommended to you, you may be less concerned about having copies of everything.

But if you are working with an "unknown quantity", you may want to make sure that the rate lock you are being promised is, in fact, real.

Whether we lock with a lender by fax or through the web, we receive a confirmation of our rate lock, the loan fee the lender is charging, and the expiration date of the lock. Any reputable lender should be willing to satisfy your concern about the terms being promised and make a copy of the rate lock available to you upon request.

Mistake No. 8: Not looking ahead to the calendar.

When you are putting your transaction together, it would be wise to look at the calendar to see how the closing date, the rate lock, and the deadline dates all fit together.

Because the standard contract in California calls for the buyer to release their financing contingency within 17 days, knowing how many working days there are to accomplish the major goals is important.

If we are going into a period where there are holidays that affect the work flow, it is easy to see how weekends and holidays can diminish the amount of time we have to get things done in a timely manner. Making sure that your real estate agent gets in touch with us at the time the contract is being negotiated will allow all of us to work together to make the transaction as low-stress as possible for all concerned.

It is always stressful when we have a buyer and seller committed to a particular closing date, the moving vans are about to be bumping into each other, and not enough forethought was given to making sure that the timeline worked for all parties.

Mistake No. 9: Expecting everything to proceed without delays.

There are many "moving parts" to successful real estate transactions. Because we are all relying on others to do their parts of the transaction, there is plenty of opportunity for delays to occur in the process.

Some of the more obvious and unpredictable reasons could include: increased work load without warning at the escrow, title company, lender, or appraisal company. We may lose precious days to meet deadlines if some key players are not available to do their part in a timely manner.

We may also encounter surprises on the credit reports with information that was previously unknown. This can create a major problem that takes a while to sort through.

The title search may pick up liens or judgments that need to be researched and cleared.

Also, the borrower or service provider may have vacation plans that we need to schedule around. Sending loan documents to another location can add 2-3 days that were not built into the process, and having other people fill in for the primary person is rarely as efficient.

There is always going to be some item that takes some extra effort and takes longer than anticipated. At the inception of your loan request we won't always know which item it will be or how much extra time it will take.

Mistake No. 10: Making major changes during the process.

As crazy as it may sound, sometimes the borrower makes some major decisions before the completion of their real estate transaction.

Some of the more damaging changes include retiring from their job or making a change to a different job. The lender will typically do a verbal verification of employment just prior to funding the loan and if the income source is gone or changed it will affect the lender's approval and could defeat the application entirely.

Also, going out and buying a car or furniture or putting any new credit in place before the closing can also create problems that cannot be solved.

If you are anticipating wanting to make changes during the process, please be sure to discuss the consequences before taking action.

If you do your best to avoid these potential mistakes, you will be in a great position to have a less stressful experience in obtaining your home loan.

Chapter 8

CLOSING COSTS AND IDEAS ON SAVING MONEY IN THE MORTGAGE PROCESS

Probably the issue that troubles borrowers the most, and that I receive the most questions about is closing costs.

In the scope of home transactions that are in the range of hundreds of thousands of dollars and sometimes millions of dollars, the closing costs represent a small percentage.

But, when a borrower looks over their Good Faith Estimate and sees a long list of fees that accumulate to several thousand dollars, it's difficult for them to make sense of what seems to be repetitive costs.

As you assess the closing costs, it is important to separate them into two categories: transactional or non-recurring charges, and recurring charges.

Transactional or non-recurring charges include:

Loan points: These are charged if you negotiate an interest rate that involves a loan origination fee and/or discount fee, and are paid to the lender. One point equals one percent of your loan amount, so let's say on a loan of $300,000 one point equals $3000.

Credit Report: You may be charged for the credit report, which goes to a credit company and is usually around $20. They pull your credit report and credit scores from Experian, TransUnion, and Equifax.

Processing Fee: Most originating lenders will have some form of processing fee. This is paid to the originating company and is for the work involved in putting together a file for presentation to the lender's underwriter. Typical processing fees are in the $500-$600 range.

Underwriting Fee: Once the file goes to the underwriting group, they have a fee for the review of the file for approval. Even if this fee is paid to the originating lender as a continuation of their process, it is not uncommon to have two distinct procedures with two distinct companies involved. This fee is paid to the underwriting company and is in the range of $400-$500.

Document Preparation: After the file is approved and it is prepared for closing, the next step is the preparation of loan documents. This fee may be paid to the lender or to a contract company for this service. The typical fee is $250-$300.

Flood Certification Fee: Additional fees that come into play include a flood certification fee of approximately $20 paid to an independent company that looks over the FEMA flood maps to determine if the property is required to have flood insurance or not.

Tax Service Fee: Also, there is a tax service fee of approximately $85, paid to an independent company, that is designed to do one of two things: If your loan has an impound account, they supply the tax bill to the lender for payment. If your loan does not have an impound account, they monitor your property so that they can inform the lender if taxes go unpaid.

Appraisal Fee: The appraisal fee is usually paid for by you at the time it is ordered. This fee is paid to an appraisal management company who chooses the appraiser from an approved panel. Their job is to ascertain the market value by comparing the home to be appraised with recently closed escrows on homes that are most similar. Typical cost is $400-$550, depending on the value of the home, and we usually arrange payment via credit card.

Escrow or Settlement Fee: The escrow or settlement agent fee is paid to the escrow company. This company is responsible for coordinating the various components of the transaction so that it closes successfully. They have to interact with the lender, the title company, insurance agent, real estate agents, notary services, homeowner's associations, attorneys, and of course the buyer and seller.

Notary Fee: Loan signing notary fee is paid to a person or company who conducts the signing of the final papers and notarizes the required forms.

Title Insurance: You provide a policy of title insurance for the benefit of the lender to insure them that they have the first lien on the property. It is paid to the title company, it is based on the loan amount, and these fees are regulated by the California Insurance Commissioner.

Sub-Escrow Fee: There may be a sub-escrow fee paid to the title company for receiving the wired loan proceeds and to be the "deep-pocket" company accountable for the funds. Escrow companies are not required to have substantial financial reserves, so the lenders are reluctant to send hundreds of thousands or millions of dollars to them. Title companies, on the other hand, have strong financial backing and are regulated by the state of California.

E-Documents: Escrow may charge you for e-document preparation. Since the final loan documents are transmitted electronically much of the time, they are charging for their time and resources to prepare the printed sets for you.

Courier Fee: Escrow may also have a need to deliver paperwork using couriers, FedEX, UPS, etc. You may see a charge for delivery fees that the escrow company collects.

Recording Fees: And, there will be a fee, paid to the counties here in California, for the recording of the deeds associated with your transaction to put them on public records.

The recurring charges will include:

Impound Account Deposit: A deposit of funds if you create an impound account for the payment of taxes and insurance.

Pro-Rata Interest: You will have pro-rated interest from the date the loan funds to the first of the following month to put the loan on a standardized 30-day billing cycle.

Hazard Insurance Premium: You will be asked to prepay your first year's property insurance premium.

Property Taxes: You may have a pro-ration of property taxes depending on whether the seller has already paid them covering the escrow closing date.

Grouping the closing costs in this manner allows you to make better comparisons between competing lending companies and loan programs, and the newly revised Good Faith Estimate you receive after applying for your loan presents the costs in this way.

So, are there any ways you can keep from spending too much on closing costs?

There are three ways and two of them go hand-in-hand:

1. Try to get the fees reduced from as many service providers as possible.

   Most of the costs enumerated above are fixed, or are a result of a formula based on purchase price and loan amount, and don't have much room for negotiation.

   Lenders' fees won't typically change because they could be accused of discriminatory lending practices if they reduce the fee for one borrower and maintain a higher fee for someone else.

   It never hurts to ask if a reduction is possible, but make sure that you get the same professional service for the reduced fee if you are successful. If you remove a person's incentive for doing a good job, you may find that your file is at the bottom of the stack for an extended period of time.

2. Don't overpay for the services that are provided in connection with your loan.

As you research getting your mortgage, you should have a good idea what is considered a normal range for the closing costs, either item-by-item or as a cumulative total.

What you want to avoid are the loan originators who have mark-ups on services provided to them. For example, credit reports are usually billed at $15-$20. If your lender charges you $50, you are over-paying for the service.

Accept the fact that there are reasonable fees for the services per-formed. But don't reward companies by doing business with them if they charging more without adding value.

3. Make sure of the suitability of mortgage product.

When you go through the mortgage process, you will probably pay a few thousand dollars for closing costs in addition to any loan origina-tion and discount points that you agree to pay.

There are times that ending your mortgage contract early and paying additional fees to refinance your loan is to your obvious benefit.

An easy example is when interest rates drop and the lower payments allow you to recover the costs of the refinance in a short period of time.

But there are times that you may feel the need to refinance and it may be beneficial, but the need should never have existed in the first place if you had been placed in a suitable loan program initially.

Before you finalize your loan decision, make sure your originator is doing a good job of understanding your needs, your goals, your risk tolerance and your time horizons. Make sure, too, that you understand how that loan fits your needs.

If you don't, you may find yourself paying repetitive fees to solve a problem that could have been avoided.

Strategies 2 & 3 are the result of finding the right person to be your mortgage provider who will care for you and treat you fairly.

Chapter 9

THE POWER OF THE PREQUALIFICATION

You've found a house that you want to buy.

You've checked other homes, you are confident in the purchase price.

You are ready to write the offer with your real estate agent.

The last time you needed a home loan, you had little difficulty getting qualified and things went smoothly.

All systems GO!

But you may need to slow down a bit.

Things have changed and the financing may not be as easy as it was the last time.

All professional real estate agents want you to go through the process of applying for a loan and getting prequalified for the likely financing you will need.

It makes every part of the process smoother.

You will have an excellent idea of the proper price range to be looking in.

You will have an idea of any obstacles that you may be facing in this new lending environment.

The agent doesn't waste time and resources showing you properties that are out of your price range.

You won't fall in love with a home that you can't afford.

The escrow period is significantly shortened if we work together to get your paperwork in order as you are looking at homes, rather than starting from scratch from day one of the escrow period.

When your offer is presented, it is strengthened by an accompanying letter from a reputable lending source, that you have done your homework and that you are prequalified for the financing.

Admittedly, there are many borrowers who find out that they are not quite prepared to buy at the time they want.

But finding that out before they spend hours looking at homes and getting emotionally attached is a good thing.

Sure, it can be disappointing. But if you are committed to buying at a future point, you can develop a game plan to solidify your career, boost your earnings, clean up some credit flaws, save more money, etc.

So if you want to put yourself in the best possible position in your next home purchase, it would be wise to follow these steps:

1. Contact your preferred lender to get your paperwork started. This will include a written loan application, supporting paperwork to verify income, assets, employment, and debts. If you work with me, it allows me to run your credit report to make sure that all is well, or to see if we have a project on our hands.

2. Narrow your choices for the type of financing vehicle you prefer. In today's world, the choices have been simplified. Low-doc, no-doc, exotic adjustable rate loans, and deferred-interest loans have essentially disappeared. The dominant choices are conventional fixed-rate, FHA, VA, some milder forms of adjustable rate loans and in some cases, interest-only programs.

3. In addition to my using my extensive experience to ascertain your qualifications, we can also obtain a decision from an automated underwriting system (AUS) that conforms to FNMA, FHLMC, FHA or VA guidelines. This system is based on data input, so the key is to know what we can verify so that we get a decision that is supportable.

4. At this point we can issue a letter indicating that we have received and reviewed your loan application, we have run your credit report and found it acceptable, and that we have verified your income, assets and debts. We can also indicate that we have a written loan approval

from the AUS that supports a specific sales price and loan amount.

5. As you find the home that fits within the qualifying criteria, we just need to make sure that the property will also be acceptable. Special care should be taken if you are looking at condominiums, or if you are looking at homes that may require some repair or remedy of deferred maintenance.

The agent representing the property and the agent representing you as a buyer will be pleased that one of the major hurdles - obtaining the financing to purchase the home - has been diligently assessed and that the surprises can be kept to a minimum.

Some borrowers dread the process of the loan application, but the reality is that it most probably will need to be done sooner or later. 'Sooner' makes the most sense to minimize transactional trauma, while 'later' backloads all the pressure when emotions are running high and deadlines are looming.

Plan ahead, work together, and make the process as smooth as possible.

Chapter 10

RISK-BASED PRICING

A big reason for the mortgage meltdown was that investors and lenders offered loan products that took on increased levels of risk.

Guidelines expanded to allow higher loans in relation to the value of the home (LTV), more permissive credit scores, and less requirement of an investment by the borrower.

As investors and lenders dropped these higher-risk programs, there has been an effort to assess risk within a more conservative framework, and it will affect your shopping for a home loan, especially by phone.

It is called risk-based pricing. And if the lender is not asking you sufficient questions, you may find that the loan quote is overly optimistic, and that you may be set up for disappointment. Let's take a look at some of the moving parts that need to be explored to provide you with reliable information:

Loan-To-Value (LTV) Ratio:

The higher the LTV is, the higher the risk is for the lender. You will find that the interest rate and loan fee combination (pricing) will be higher for the higher risk categories. For example, if the loan is 60% LTV or less, the pricing is very favorable. There will be incremental increases in the loan fee charged at a specific interest rate if the loan request falls between 60%-65%, 65%-70%, 70%-75%, and 75%-80%.

If the loan request is higher than 80%, the lender will typically require private mortgage insurance. This mortgage insurance is for the lender's benefit and gives them the feeling of comfort they need in order to offer loans above 80% because they now will have insurance for that risk.

Credit Scores:

When we obtain a credit report, we usually are able to obtain information and scores from the three major bureaus: Equifax, TransUnion and Experian. The lender will usually use the middle of the three scores for evaluation purposes.

In today's market, a score above 740 will allow us to fit the request within the most favorable pricing model. As with the LTV model, there will be incremental increases in the loan fee for a specific interest rate if the score falls between 720-739, 700-719, 680-699, 660-679, 640-659, and 620-639.

Loan Points:

In the past, before the mortgage market upheaval, it was common for lenders to offer "no point" or even "no point, no cost" loans.

The market factored in a value for interest rate changes. On a 30-year fixed rate loan, a good rule of thumb used to be that for adding a loan fee of .50 points, you could save .125% in interest rate. This scale worked in both directions, so that if you wanted to do a "no point" loan, your loan would be approximately .25% higher than if you were willing to pay 1.0 point in loan fee.

In today's environment, lenders are assessing higher risk to loans where the borrower puts as little into the transaction as possible. Lenders are no longer willing to offer "no point" loans with such a small differential to the interest rate. As an example, let's say an interest rate of 5.0% is available at a loan fee of 1.0 points, but to obtain a "no point" loan the rate is at 5.50%. So, the market is saying that .125% in interest rate is only worth about .25 points in loan fee. This quote is based on a credit score of 740, with a LTV of 80% or less.

Property Considerations:

A single-family detached home is considered by the lenders as having the lowest risk.

A condominium, because of the nature of the common ownership in the project, has a higher risk associated with it. Actions and decisions by other homeowners in the project can affect your unit value or the need for special assessments to pay for community obligations and repairs.

Buying a 2-4 unit property is also considered higher risk, because the buyer is typically relying on the ongoing income from the adjoining units to be able to make the monthly mortgage payments.

Summary:

When you combine these factors, there is a huge range of interest rate and fee quotes that a borrower could encounter.

Loan requests of 80% with a credit score of 630 will be significantly higher than a 60% loan with a credit score of 740. If you are not advised of this information when you are doing your loan research, there is every likelihood that the interest rate and fee that is finalized for you will be more expensive than the original "quote".

So, if you are hopeful to take advantage of these favorable interest rates, especially for loans that are eligible for sale to FNMA and FHLMC, don't wait too long to explore your options. A new 30-year or 15-year fixed rate loan could improve your finances going forward, and may allow you the opportunity to get away from an adjustable rate loan that will be coming up for recast in the near future.

A small investment of time to get paperwork started will allow you to discuss locking in the loan.

CHAPTER 11

LEARNING FROM OTHERS

A couple of years ago, I did a fund-raising charity bicycle ride for the benefit of United Cerebral Palsy in San Diego.

At the post-ride dinner, I was talking with another rider and when she found out that I was a mortgage broker, she asked me a number of questions and I learned about her predicament.

She had worked through another mortgage originator previously.

She had her existing loan for about a year and a half. She discovered, too late, that it was one that allowed for deferred interest or "negative amortization". This loan was a refinance due to a divorce situation, so she pulled cash out of the property to pay off her former spouse.

At that time, she financed 90% of the value of the home, and she was qualified based on the "stated income" program.

She had a strong credit history and credit score, but limited savings or retirement funds, so she needed every advantage to qualify for the new loan and keep her condominium for herself and her two children.

And in the "Add Insult to Injury" Department, she also had a prepayment penalty on the loan that was not made clear to her.

She could be the Poster Girl for the excesses that had taken place in liberal underwriting and approvals, and also how misplaced trust in financial advisors can create bigger problems.

Let's look closely at some of these details.

First, she was emotionally attached to wanting to keep her condominium for comfort and security and that framed her decision-making at every turn. She never seriously considered selling the home and splitting the proceeds with her former spouse because she didn't want to rent or downsize to a smaller home.

She needed her loan originator to have been bluntly honest with her about the decision she was facing.

Second, the low payments that the deferred interest option loan offered were very attractive to her, and were affordable.

Although she seemed to recall having some of the consequences of that loan explained to her, she never thoroughly understood how it worked.

When she got the loan, the amount of interest deferral was modest, but as interest rates had increased she was looking at her loan balance increasing significantly each month.

The loan allowed for the principal balance to increase no higher than 110% of the original loan amount. When the loan began the projection was that it would not happen for many years, but with the higher interest deferral she was facing significantly higher payments within the next year.

She needed her mortgage originator to have gone through the worst-case scenario with her to make sure that it was manageable and acceptable to her.

Third, she obtained her loan, and bought out her ex-husband near the top of the real estate market. Property values had dropped, and combined with her loan balance increasing, her equity was being squeezed very close to nothing.

She needed to have been directed to a real estate professional who could counsel her on the wisdom of buying out her ex-husband or to make the decision to sell the property instead.

Fourth, by relying on the "stated income" qualifying feature, she allowed herself to be put into a situation that could become increasingly unaffordable. I did not get all the details of what she really made versus what was represented on her loan submission, but she may have been optimistic about having additional income that did not come to fruition.

She needed her mortgage originator to have been thorough with her to make sure that the income she was relying upon was stable enough to keep the obligations affordable for her.

Lastly, the prepayment penalty handcuffed her to the existing loan unless she wanted to pay thousands of dollars to get out of it. Of course, she did not have the equity in the property or the cash in reserves to absorb this kind of expense.

She needed her mortgage originator to have been clear about the features of the loan and what the financial consequences of those features would be to her.

What can we learn from her ordeal?

A. Seek out many solutions to the problem and don't rule out any of them until you have a chance to assess the merits of all of them.

There is a saying that when your only tool is a hammer, you treat everything like a nail. But be cautious that the person from whom you are seeking advice is helping you brainstorm solutions to your problem and not just promoting their product.

In too many cases, if you speak with a real estate agent, they will want you to list the house with them. If you speak with a mortgage originator, they want to sell you a new loan.

But there are quality professionals in both industries that will give you honest advice and resources to explore to make sure that you are well-cared for.

B. Thoroughly understand why the proposal that is being offered is good for you, and take the time to understand the details.

The mortgage business can be confusing, and some originators are not well-skilled on explaining the features without using verbal shorthand, so it is imperative that you insist that they keep explaining it until you understand it properly. If they are unable to communicate with you effectively, you should find someone who can. The consequences of misunderstandings or failures to disclose pertinent terms to you are just too expensive in both dollars and emotional distress.

C. Forecast what the "worst-case scenario" is, especially if you are considering an adjustable rate loan. We can make projections based on reasonable assumptions, but insist on knowing how the loan performs if everything goes crazy.

That is the only way that you can satisfy yourself that you have a plan that can work for you no matter what.

At the risk of being repetitive, it is important that you find the right people to counsel you, and who are truly looking out for your best interests.

If my bicycle-riding acquaintance had followed up with me after that dinner to help brainstorm a solution to her problem, I would have done my best to help her. When you come to me for help, advice, or mortgage services you can be confident that I will do the same for you.

FINAL THOUGHTS

I hope that you found the information in this book valuable and helpful.

It comes from my experiences in over 30 years in the mortgage lending business. Because guidelines and regulations create changes in the mortgage business, it is important that you align yourself with a professional who researches appropriate solutions for you.

As you work toward purchasing your home, or to change the terms of your loan to something more suitable through a refinance, I wish you success in meeting your financing goals.

GLOSSARY

APR
: The Annual Percentage Rate gives the borrower a basis for comparing competing interest rate and fee quotes by taking into account the effect of the finance charges expressed as an effective interest rate.

AUS
: An Automated Underwriting System is a web-based program available to mortgage lenders. With proper data input, it renders an underwriting decision based on the compatibility of the loan request to FNMA and FHLMC guidelines.

CLTV
: Combined Loan to Value ratio is the comparison of the loan amounts on the first loan plus the second loan in relation to the value of the home. For example, a first loan amount of $300,000 combined with a second loan amount of $100,000 on a property valued at $500,000 represents a CLTV of 80%.

FHA
: The Federal Housing Administration is part of the Department of Housing and Urban Development. FHA provides a system for insurance of loans with lesser down payments.

FHLMC
: Known as "Freddie Mac", the Federal Home Loan Mortgage Corporation was created in 1970 as a Government Sponsored Enterprise to purchase loans from lenders and provide liquidity to the mortgage market.

FICO Scores
: FICO stands for Fair Isaac Corporation and has become

the generic label applied to credit scoring models.

Through proprietary modeling, each of the three credit repositories – Experian, TransUnion, and Equifax – produce scores ranging from 300 to 850. Higher scores are designed to be predictive of more credit-worthy borrowers.

FNMA   Known as "Fannie Mae", the Federal National Mortgage Association was created in 1938 as a Government Sponsored Enterprise to purchase loans from lenders and provide liquidity to the mortgage market.

GFE   The Good Faith Estimate is a required disclosure from lenders to the borrower, and is to be provided within 3 business days from receipt of a loan application. It's purpose is to provide an estimate of fees and costs in obtaining the home loan.

LTV   Loan to Value ratio is the comparison of the loan amount on the first loan in relation to the value of the home. For example, a loan amount of $400,000 on a property valued at $500,000 represents an 80% LTV

Point(s)   A point equals 1 percent of the loan amount. For example, on a loan amount of $200,000, one point equals $2,000. When interest rates are quoted there is often an origination fee disclosed based on a certain number of points.

Pricing   Refers to the combination of interest rate and origination fee quoted on your transaction. For example, you may hear pricing models such as 4.5% with a loan fee of 1 point (see above) or 4.75% with a loan fee of zero points.

TIL   The Truth-In-Lending disclosure is designed to show the borrower an effective interest rate based on the combination of interest rate and finance charges. The most significant part of the disclosure is the Annual Percentage Rate.

VA   The Home Loan Guaranty division of the Department of Veterans Affairs guarantees home loans to lenders for loans made to eligible veterans. Loans made under this program often allow the veteran to purchase a home with no down payment.

An Incredible Free Gift For You

(Hundreds of Dollars of Free Information For You and a Special Bonus!)

Go to www.DougBrennecke.com and sign up for my special report:

"SEVEN STRATEGIES TO HELP YOU AVOID HEADACHES AND SAVE MONEY IN THE MORTGAGE PROCESS".

You will also be registered for receiving my bi-weekly electronic news-letter that provides:

- Basic mortgage education
- Thoughts and opinions on the mortgage business
- Updates on recent developments

The website provides Archived Articles, Audio, Videos, Success Stories, and Product Offerings. Take advantage of these valuable resources to help you Win The Mortgage Game!

Special Bonus: My Gift of Appreciation

When you go to the website, select the Contact Doug page and complete the web form. Provide your e-mail address and let me know that you purchased this book and I will send you a recording of a 33-minute radio interview done for "The Very Best Job In The World"!